Mediterranean Diet Cookbook

The Most famous Salads and Starters Recipes

Contents

Introduction

Mediterranean diet is based on vegetables, fruits, herbs, nuts, beans and whole grains. Meals are built around these plant-based foods. Moderate amounts of dairy, poultry and eggs are also central to the Mediterranean Diet, as is seafood. In contrast, red meat is eaten only occasionally.

In this cookbook, you will find the most famous healthy Mediterranean diet salads and starters recipes. Most of them are based on products you can likely find at your local specialty grocery store. To reduce prep time, you can use presleasoned grilled meat and chicken from the refrigerated section, bottled balsamic vinaigrette and a few other ready-to-use ingredients to make these quick, simple, affordable, and delicious salads.

The Green Salad

There are many different appellations for this salad. Some call it the *Local Salad,* others call it the *Green Salad.* It is usually served as a side dish or with sandwiches.

Ingredients:

2 green bell pepper, finely chopped
3 medium cucumbers, finely chopped
3 medium tomatoes, finely chopped
½ cup green onions, finely chopped
¼ cup fresh parsley
1 clove garlic, minced
6 red radishes, finely chopped (optional)
2 Tbsp. olive oil
2 Tbsp. lemon juice
Salt and pepper

Directions:

- Mix the tomatoes, green bell pepper, cucumbers, parsley, green onions, garlic, and red radishes.
- Whisk the olive oil and the lemon juice and season with salt and pepper. Add the mixture to the salad before serving.
- This is the essential green salad and it can be added to onion rings and chunks of white cheese and olives. Different dressings can be used for the presentation.

Picture 1: The Green Salad

Roasted Eggplant Salad

Ingredients:

2 Italian eggplants
2 large potatoes
1 green bell pepper
1 large red onion
2 Tbsp. garlic, minced
2 Tbsp. fresh parsley, chopped
1 tsp. ground cumin
¼ cup olive oil
1 Tbsp. red vinegar
1 Tbsp. lemon juice
½ cup tahini
Salt and pepper

Directions:

- In a pot, boil the potatoes until fully cooked. Cut into (2 ½ cm) thick rounds.
- Roast the whole eggplant, uncut, on direct fire, over medium-high heat or in the oven at 350°F (180°C), turning occasionally until the skin is completely roasted on all sides.
- Peel the skin and cut in half discarding as many seeds as possible.
- Chop the eggplants into cubes. Add the lemon juice to avoid discoloration and set aside.
- Roast whole the green bell pepper on direct fire over medium-high heat or in the oven at 350°F (180°C) turning occasionally until the skin is completely roasted.
- Remove from oven and wrap it with a plastic wrap for 5 minutes. Remove plastic wrap. Cut in half, peel the skin, discard the seeds and chop into small cubes.
- In a sauté pan, add 2 Tbsp of olive oil and add the chopped red onions for 10 minutes or until golden brown.
- Mix red onions, the eggplant, parsley, green bell pepper, and tahini well. Season with spices, salt and pepper.

- For making the cumin dressing, combine the minced garlic with the rest of the olive oil, and the ground cumin in a small bowl.
- Arrange the potato rounds on a serving plate drizzling with some olive oil, garlic, and cumin dressing and spoon the eggplant mixture in the middle.

Note:

The olive oil, garlic, and cumin dressing can be used on other types of salad or as a marinade.

Picture 2: The Roasted Eggplant Salad

Toasted Bread Salad

Ingredients:

2 loaves of Arabic Pita Bread
3 medium cucumbers, peeled, seeded and chopped
3 tomatoes, seeded and finely diced
1 clove garlic, minced
2 Tbsp. olive oil
¼ cup fresh mint leaves, chopped
½ cup green onions
2 Tbsp. olive oil
1 tsp. dry mint
1 heart romaine lettuce
Salt and pepper

Directions:

- Cut the bread into small pieces. Spray with olive oil and garlic. Toast in a 350°F (180°C) oven or on stove top until golden brown.
- Mix the tomatoes with the cucumber, onions, and fresh mint.
- Whisk the olive oil and vinegar well and season with salt, pepper and dry mint.
- Arrange lettuce leaves in a fan shape on a serving plate.
- Combine the toasted bread, the vegetable mixture, and olive oil dressing.
- Spoon the salad on top of the bed of lettuce immediately before serving.

Note: Sumac, tuna or anchovy can be added to this salad.

Tabbouleh

Tabbouleh is a seasoned bulgur and parsley salad. The name is derived from the Arabic phrase translated as "spice mixture."

Ingredients:

½ cup fine bulgur wheat
8 green onions (scallions, spring onions), white parts only, finely chopped
1 big tomato, finely diced
4 cups parsley, stems removed, finely chopped
1/3 cup lemon juice
¼ tsp. ground cinnamon
1/3 tsp. ground cumin
1/8 tsp. ground red pepper
4 Tbsp. olive oil
1/3 cup fresh mint, finely chopped
2 hearts romaine lettuce
Salt and black pepper to taste

Directions:

• Pick stones from bulk bulgur before using. Rinse with cold water. Drain and set aside.
• Rinse the parsley and pat dry before chopping.
• In a medium bowl, combine all the ingredients except the lettuce and mint.
• Let the salad stand in the refrigerator for 1 hour to absorb the flavors.
• Add the finely chopped mint before serving.
• Toss and taste for extra seasoning.
• Serve on a bed of lettuce.

Note:

There are four types of bulgur:
- The first type is a coarse grind, used in soups, pilafs, and cooked dishes.
- The second type is a less coarse grind, used as stuffing and in baked dishes and casseroles.
- The third type is a medium grind, used as crust in *kubba* and *kufta*.

- And the fourth type is a fine grind, used in salads as well as *kufta*. Bulgur has the unique ability of absorbing flavors. It can be soaked by adding any favorite ingredient such as a chopped onion, tomato juice, or any kind of stock before using.

Picture 3: Tabbouleh

Fresh Fava Beans Salad

Ingredients:

1 medium onion, chopped
8 artichoke hearts, fresh, canned or frozen
3 Tbsp. olive oil
2 cloves garlic, minced
1 lb. (½ kg) fresh fava beans, skinned
1 lb. (½ kg) green peas
2 Tbsp. fresh dill, chopped
2 Tbsp. fresh mint, chopped
1 tsp. lemon juice
¼ cup water
Salt and pepper

Directions:

- In a sauté pan, heat the oil over medium-high heat. Sauté the onions for 8 minutes or until golden brown, stirring occasionally.
- Add the garlic and cook for 4 more minutes. Combine the artichoke hearts, fava beans, and green peas. Blanch the artichoke and green peas if fresh and simply rinse them if frozen.
- Toss in the greens, season with salt and pepper adding lemon juice and water.
  Cover and simmer over medium-high heat for about 10 minutes or until soft.
- Garnish the salad with rings of sliced tomatoes before serving.

Note:

It is preferable to prepare this salad several hours before serving.

Sharmoula Salad

This salad is served with Fish meals, it's a well-known salad from the Moroccan cuisine.

Ingredients:

8 tomatoes, seeded, and chopped
1 green bell pepper
1 red bell pepper
2 cloves garlic
2 Tbsp. olive oil
½ tsp. ground cumin
½ tsp. ground red hot pepper
Salt and pepper

Directions:

- Spray some oil on the red and green bell peppers and roast on a direct fire or in a 350°F (180°C) oven until the skins become brown.
- Remove from oven and wrap the peppers in plastic wrap for 6 minutes. Discard the plastic wrap. Seed, peel skin and finely chop.
- In a pan, heat the oil over medium-high heat. Add the garlic, tomatoes, and season with salt and pepper. Simmer for 30 minutes on low heat until much of the tomato juice evaporates. Combine the roasted peppers and mix well. Simmer for 5 more minutes and serve.

Picture 4: Sharmoula Salad

Kushary Salad

Ingredients:

2 large tomatoes
1 cup chickpeas, cooked
¼ cup red onions, finely chopped
2 Tbsp. fresh cilantro, chopped
2 Tbsp. olive oil
2 Tbsp. lemon juice
Salt and pepper

Directions:

- Finely chop the tomatoes.
- If the chickpeas are canned, rinse them with hot water. If frozen, soak in hot water. If dry rinse and boil 1 cup of chickpeas to 5 cups of water. Cook until the chickpeas are soft. Drain and set aside to cool.
- In a bowl, toss chickpeas, tomatoes, onions, cilantro, olive oil, and lemon juice. Season with salt and pepper to taste.
- Cover securely and refrigerate to combine the flavors before serving.

Note:

- This salad is similar to sauce. It can be served on the side of pasta dishes or rice.
- You can serve a dressing of tomato juice, lemon juice, and olive oil as a condiment to many main dishes.

Green Black Eyed Pea Salad

Ingredients:

1 cup green black eyed peas
3 cups water
¼ cup red onions, chopped
¼ tsp. red hot pepper
½ Tbsp. fresh cilantro, chopped
2 Tbsp. olive oil
2 Tbsp. red vinegar
Salt and pepper

Directions:

- Soak the green black eyed peas in hot water for 30 minutes. Rinse well and drain.
- In a saucepan, add water to the green black eyed peas over medium-high heat and bring to a boil. Reduce heat and simmer for 45 minutes or until soft.
- In a pan, combine the oil and vinegar and bring to a boil. Add the red onions and cook until soft. Remove from heat and set aside to cool.
- In a bowl, combine the green black eyed peas, cooked red onions, olive oil, vinegar, chopped cilantro and season with salt and pepper.
- Spoon the salad into securely coved bowl and refrigerate for several hours before serving.

Note: This salad can be slightly heated before serving. Vinegar can be substituted for lemon juice.

Picture 5: Green Black Eyed Pea Salad

Baba Ganouge " Metabbal"

This salad is called *"Metabbal"* in the Levant (Middle East) and *"Baba Ganouge"* in Egypt. Eggplant is the salad's main ingredient.

Ingredients:

1 Italian eggplant
1 medium onion
2 Tbsp. lemon juice
½ cup tahini
½ cup warm water
4 Tbsp. plain yogurt
4 Tbsp. olive oil

To garnish:
Pomegranate
seeds
1 lemon, sliced
Parsley, finely chopped

Directions:

- Preheat oven to 350°F (180°C).
- Rinse the eggplant well and pat dry. Prick the eggplant all over using the end of a sharp knife.
- Rub the eggplant and onion with olive oil and place them on roasting pan. Roast for 30 minutes or until the skin of the eggplant is black and the flesh is soft.
- While the eggplant is still hot, wrap well with plastic wrap and leave for 2 minutes. Cut off the stem with the knife. Peel the skin and remove as many seeds as possible.
- Using a fork, mash the eggplant, adding lemon juice to prevent discoloration. Set aside. Finely chop the roasted onion.
- In a deep bowl, whisk tahini with warm water and add the yogurt and 3 Tbsp. of olive oil. Season with salt and black pepper to taste.
- Add the eggplant and chopped onion to the tahini mixture. Whisk to combine evenly.

- Garnish with olive oil, pomegranate seeds, lemon slices, and finely chopped parsley before serving.

Notes:

- It is better to choose a glossy, dark purple colored eggplant with a smooth and firm skin. It is also important to pick a male eggplant rather than a female eggplant because the former tends to have less seeds and less bitter. In doing so, look at the indentation at the bottom. "If it is deep and shaped like a dash, it's female. If it is shallow and round, it's male." *Source: The Cook's Thesaurus, by Lori Alden.*
- *Baba Ganouge* can be kept in a tightly-covered container the refrigerator for two days.

Picture 6: Baba Ganouge "Metabbal"

Humous: Chickpeas Spread

Ingredients:

1 ½ cups dry chickpeas
½ cup tahini
¼ cup warm water
2 Tbsp. lemon juice
2 Tbsp. olive oil
1 tsp. cumin powder
1 clove garlic (optional)
Salt and white pepper

For garnish:
Whole chickpeas and chopped parsley

Directions:

- Rinse chickpeas well. Soak in water for 24 hours, changing water every few hours.
- In a saucepan, bring 3 cups of water to a boil over medium-high heat. Add the chickpeas and return to a boil, then reduce heat and simmer.
- Simmer the chickpeas until soft, skimming off any impurities that rise to the surface. This should take around 1 ½ hours. The water should cover the chickpeas as they are cooking; add more if necessary. Once the chickpeas are done, drain
and set aside to cool.
- Peel chickpeas and blend in a food processer. Add tahini, garlic, lemon juice, and olive oil. Season the mixture with salt, white pepper, and cumin, processing on high until the mixture is soft and well combined. Add a tablespoon or two of extra water if the mixture is thick.
- Garnish with whole chickpeas and chopped parsley just before serving.

Notes:

- Boiled chickpeas and the water used to cook them can be had as a hot drink after adding cumin, lemon, and hot chili pepper.
- Canned chickpeas can be substituted in this recipe after rinsing thoroughly and draining.

- The quantity of tahini can be varied depending on its thickness and brand.
- Chickpeas are a very good source of protein.
- You can Substitute 2 ½ cups of canned chickpeas for every cup of dry chickpeas.

Picture 7: Humous (Chickpeas Spread)

Muhammara: Red Pepper Spread

This is called *Muhammara* because it contains red pepper. It can be served as an appetizer or as a sauce for white or red meat.

Ingredients:

1 onion, finely chopped
2 medium red bell peppers, chopped
2 medium tomatoes, chopped
3 Tbsp. olive oil
4 cloves garlic
3 Tbsp. pomegranate molasses
3 Tbsp. tomato paste
3 slices of bread, toasted in the oven or a toaster
½ cup almonds, roasted
½ cup cashews, roasted (optional)
1 fresh red chili pepper, seeded
Nutmeg for garnish

Directions:

- Heat 2 Tbsp. of olive oil over medium heat. Sauté garlic for 2 minutes or until golden brown.
- Add onions and cook, stirring occasionally for 3 minutes. Mix in the red pepper, tomatoes, and 2 Tbsp. of pomegranate molasses.
- Add the tomato paste. Cook for about 15 minutes, stirring occasionally. When it is done, remove from heat and set aside to cool.
- Place the toast in a food processor and pulse on medium speed until it becomes a fine powder. Mix in almonds, cashews, and red chili pepper. Pulse until finely ground. Set a cup of the mixture aside.
- Combine the tomato mixture and bread crumb mixture, and pulse in the food processor until well combined. Season with salt and pepper to taste.
- The consistency of the *Muhammra* can be adjusted by adding water or reserved bread crumb mixture.
- Garnish with nutmeg, olive oil, and pomegranate molasses before serving.

Yogurt Salad

It is one of the easiest salads to prepare. It also can be served with other dishes.

Ingredients:

1 cup plain yogurt
2 medium cucumbers
1 clove garlic
½ tsp. dry mint
1 Tbsp. olive oil
Salt and pepper

Directions:

- Pour the yogurt into a cheesecloth bag. Set aside for no more than 2 hours to drain.
- Rinse the cucumbers. Peel and grate or chop the cucumber. Squeeze lightly to get rid of the water.
- In a bowl, combine the yogurt with the other ingredients. Season with salt and pepper to taste.
- Cover and keep in the refrigerator for several hours to allow the yogurt to absorb the flavors before serving.

Notes:

- Dry dill or ground cumin can be substituted for the mint.
- Chopped green onions can be added.

Tahini Dip

Ingredients:

1 clove garlic
½ tsp. ground cumin
½ tsp. ground black pepper
½ cup tahini
¼ cup water
¼ cup lemon juice
1 tsp. salt

Directions:

- Pound the garlic with salt in a mortar and pestle. Add the cumin and pepper.
- Whisk tahini and water together and stir in the lemon juice.
- Stir in the garlic and spice paste to the tahini mixture.

Notes:

-This salad can be used as a sauce or a dressing for green salad or other types of salad.

-It is preferable to prepare the salad ahead of time to blend the flavors. You can also use a food processor to prepare this recipe. When cooking with tahini, it is helpful to rest the jar in a bain-marie (water bath), stirring to get the paste and oil together.

-To make Baba *Ganoush*, one cup of this salad can be mixed with one cup of yogurt and two roasted mashed eggplants. To make *Hummus*, combine 1 cup of cooked chickpeas with 1 cup of this recipe in a food processor.

-To make *Shawarma* sauce, add 1 tsp. red hot pepper, 2 Tbsp. chopped parsley, and ½ cup of finely diced tomatoes to tahini salad.

Lentil Soup

Lentils are high in nutritional value, they can be served as a main course.

Ingredients:

2 cups dry lentils, red or yellow
5 Tbsp. vegetable oil
1 large onion, chopped
1 large carrot, peeled, and minced
1 stalk celery, finally chopped
2 cloves garlic
8 cups stock (chicken or meat)
1 tsp. ground cumin
1 small onion, sliced
1 Tbsp. lemon juice
Salt and pepper

Directions:

- Rinse the lentils well.
- In a pot, add 3 Tbsp. of oil over medium-high heat and sauté the chopped onions, carrots, celery, and garlic for 10 minutes.
- Add the stock and lentils and bring to a boil.
- Reduce the heat and simmer for about 45-60 minutes.
- When the lentils are soft, combine the salt, pepper, and cumin.
- Reduce the heat to low and simmer for 10 more minutes to combine the flavors.
- Remove from heat. Transfer to a food processor and blend well until smooth.
- In a sauté pan, add 2 Tbsp. of oil over medium-high heat and combine the sliced onion until golden brown.
- Transfer the sliced and caramelized onions to a plate lined with paper towels.
- Garnish the lentils soup with lemon juice, and caramelized onions before serving.

Note:

Vegetable stock can be used as a substitute for chicken or meat stock. Water can also be used as a substitute, but it will taste differently in this case.

Picture 8: Lentil Soup

Alharirah Soup

This soup is served in ten different ways. Each had a different mouthwatering preparation.

Ingredients:

½ cup whole brown lentils
1 cup chickpeas, cooked or canned
½ cup all-purpose flour
1 cup medium onion
½ cup fresh cilantro
1 large tomato
¼ cup fresh parsley leaves
4 stalks celery
2 Tbsp. olive oil
2 Tbsp. tomato paste
½ tsp. ground black pepper
½ tsp. salt
1 tsp. ground cinnamon
½ tsp. ground ginger
1 ¼ lbs. (½ kg) beef, cut into small chunks
10 cups water

Directions:

- Blend the onion, fresh cilantro, tomato, fresh parsley, and celery until the mixture becomes a smooth liquid.
- In a pot, heat the oil over medium-high heat. Add the mixture and tomato paste and season with salt, stirring occasionally.
- Combine the meat chunks and cover. Simmer over medium-high heat until the meat is fully cooked. Add 9 cups of water reserving the last cup.
- Add the lentils and chickpeas, (if the chickpeas were dry, soak and boil until soft).
- When the soup starts to stew, mix the all-purpose flour with the reserved cup of water to a paste, gradually pour in the soup, stirring occasionally.

Note:

If canned chickpeas are used, don't add until 5 minutes before the soup is done.
This soup can be prepared in many different ways.
Dry rice or uncooked short vermicelli can be added before the soup is fully cooked.
Also, chickpeas can be substituted with white beans or any other type of beans.
You can also substitute any of the vegetables with vegetables of your choice.

Picture 9: Alharirah Soup

Spinach Soup (Chards)

Ingredients:

2 ¼ lbs. (1 kg) chards or spinach
1 cup rice, cooked
1 tomato
1 Tbsp. olive oil
1 medium onion, chopped
8 cups stock (chicken, meat, or vegetable)
1 egg
½ cup plain yogurt
¼ cup parmesan cheese, shredded
Salt and pepper

Directions:

- Heat the oil over medium-high heat and caramelize the onions for 5 minutes.
- Rinse the spinach well and pat dry. Add the spinach to the onions and stir until wilted.
- With a slotted spoon, remove spinach from the pan and chop finely. Transfer to a saucepan and over medium-high heat.
- Set ½ cup of stock aside. Add the rest of the stock to the spinach and bring to a boil.
- In a bowl, beat the egg well.
- Add the reserved ½ cup of stock with ½ cup of plain yogurt to the beaten egg. Mix well and gradually pour into the spinach pan, stirring.
- Add the rice. It is important at this point not allow the mixture to boil. Season with salt and pepper.
- Peel, seed, and finely chop the tomatoes.
- Garnish with shredded parmesan cheese and chopped tomatoes. Serve hot.

Note: Any type of fresh leafy greens can be used to make this dish.

Picture 10: Spinach Soup

Cumin Soup

As a substitute for beef and cumin, chicken and coriander can be used to prepare this soup.

Ingredients:

1 ¼ lbs. (½ kg) beef, cut into chunks
1 ¼ lbs. (½ kg) lean lamb, boneless, cut into chunks
1 Tbsp. freshly ground cumin
2 Tbsp. all-purpose flour
2 Tbsp. butter
1 medium onion, minced
8 ½ cups water
1 cup mushrooms, chopped
1 cup uncooked couscous, or ½ cup cooked rice
2 hot peppers, finely chopped
Salt and pepper

Directions:

- Rinse the meat well and pat dry.
- In a small bowl, mix the salt, pepper, cumin, and all-purpose flour. Rub the meat with the mixture.
- Heat 1 Tbsp. of butter over medium-high heat and sauté the onions until golden brown.
- Add the meat and mix, cover, reduce heat, and simmer for 15 minutes.
- Pour in the water and simmer until the meat is almost done.
- Add the mushrooms and continue cook until the meat is fully cooked.
- In a separate saucepan off the heat, combine the couscous with one cup of boiling water. Cover tightly and let stand for 10 minutes. Fluff the couscous with a fork.
- Add the couscous or cooked rice to the cumin soup and garnish with chopped hot pepper.

Note:

This dish is famous for the fragrant flavor of cumin. Therefore, it is important to use freshly ground cumin. Roast the cumin in a dry pan over medium-high heat or in a hot oven, just until it becomes fragrant. Grind well in a spice or coffee grinder.

Sumac and Fava Beans Soup

This soup infuses fava beans with the distinctive and delicious flavor of sumac.

Ingredients:

4 tomatoes, quartered
1 medium onion, cut into rings
2 cloves garlic
1 green bell pepper, sliced into wedges
4 Tbsp. olive oil
½ cup cooked fava beans
2 Tbsp. sumac
2 tsp. ground cumin
¼ tsp. black pepper
1 Tbsp. fresh cilantro or fresh parsley, chopped
Salt
8 cups of water

Directions:

- In a roasting pan, combine the onions, garlic, and pepper and Spray with olive oil. Roast in a 375°F (190°C) oven for 20 minutes.
- Toss the vegetables and roast for 10 more minutes, until golden brown.
- Remove from the oven and set aside to cool.
- Add some water to the same roasting pan and bring to a boil on the stove, scraping off the flavorful bits stuck to the bottom of the pan. Set aside.
- In a food processor, blend the onions and garlic well.
- Finely chop the bell pepper and tomatoes.
- Add the rest of the water to the fava beans and season with sumac and cumin. Cover securely and simmer over low heat until fully cooked.
- In a bowl, combine water from roasting pan, onions, garlic, pepper, and tomatoes.
- Add this mixture to the fava beans and stir well. Season with salt and pepper and simmer for 10 minutes.
- Garnish with freshly chopped parsley or cilantro when serving.

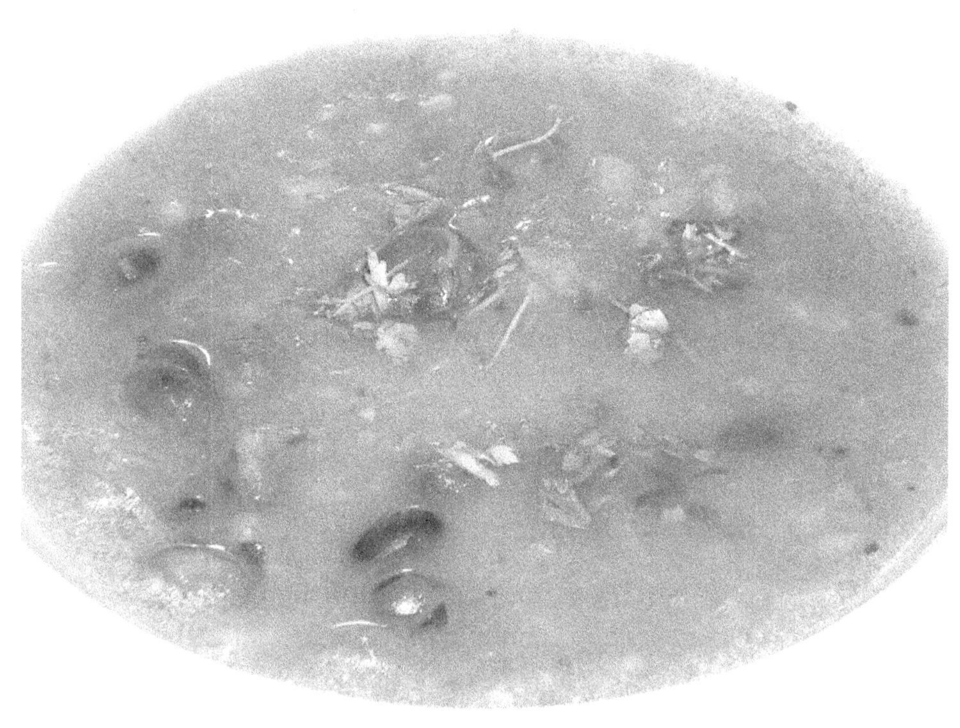

Picture 11: Fava Beans Soup

Chickpeas Soup

The chickpea discs in this dish can be stuffed with meat and it can be treated as a full meal.

Ingredients:

1 cup dry chickpeas
1 large onion
1 ¼ lbs. (½ kg) ground beef or lamb
1 tsp. allspice
Salt
8 cups chicken stock
1 ¼ lbs. (½ kg) spinach

Directions:

- Rinse the chickpeas well. Pat dry and grind.
- In a food processer, blend the onions until they become a liquid. Add the chickpeas and continue blending until the mixture becomes smooth.
- Add the ground beef to the mixture and process until well combined.
- Season with allspice and salt to taste.
- Form the mixture into medium-sized discs about 2″ (5 cm) in diameter and ½″ (1 ½ cm) thick.
- In a pot, add the chickpea discs and enough chicken stock to cover them. Cover securely and cook until done, about 20 minutes. Alternatively, you could steam the chickpea discs.
- Rinse the spinach well and chop horizontally.
- In another pot, heat the stock over medium-high heat. Bring to a boil and add the spinach. Season with salt.
- Place the chickpea discs in a serving bowl, and pour the soup and spinach on top.

Note:

- The chickpea discs can be stuffed with meat just like *Kubba*.
- Chickpeas were grown by the ancient Egyptians and Romans. Chickpeas have been used ever since and they are now the fourth most consumed grain, after wheat, rice, and corn.
67% of the calories in chickpeas come from carbohydrates, and 12.8% come from proteins.

Picture 12: Chickpeas Soup

Whole Wheat Soup

This soup is served in the Gulf region, but with a different name, *Jerrish*. It is cooked differently in the Gulf region than the recipe.

Ingredients:

2 onions cut into rings
2 cloves garlic, minced
2 Tbsp. oil
2 stalks cinnamon
4 cloves cardamom
5 cloves whole black pepper
½ cup whole wheat berries
5 cup chicken or meat stock
5 cups water
1 tsp. salt
2 Tbsp. fresh parsley, chopped
1 Tbsp. lemon juice
1 lb. (½ kg) chunks of cooked meat (optional)

Directions:

- Heat the oil over medium-high heat. Add the onions and garlic stirring occasionally until slightly golden.
- Combine the water, cinnamon, cardamom, and black pepper. Simmer over medium-high heat for 20 minutes until the onions are translucent.
- Rinse the whole wheat well and drain, grind in a food processor to fine powder and add it to the chicken or meat stock. Cook over medium-high heat and bring to a boil. Reduce the heat and simmer until fully cooked, stirring occasionally. Add more water if necessary.
- Combine the onions and wheat mixture and season with salt.
- Add the chopped parsley and lemon juice after the wheat is well done.
- Discard the cinnamon stalks, whole cardamom, and whole black pepper before serving.

Note:

Meat bones can be used in preparing this dish instead of meat chunks. In this case, water can be used as a substitute for chicken or meat stock. Also, whole wheat flour can be used instead of whole wheat berries. This might take longer cooking time. This should be cooked over medium-high heat, stirring intermittently so the wheat doesn't stick to the bottom of the pot.

Picture 13: Whole Wheat Soup

Vegetable and Vermicelli Soup

This soup can be prepared with chicken and rice instead, following the same steps.

Ingredients:

1 red bell pepper, finely chopped
1 zucchini, finely chopped
1 large carrots, peeled and finely chopped
2 tomatoes, finely chopped
2 tsp. fresh cilantro, chopped
¼ cup onions, finely chopped
2 ¼ lbs. (1 kg) beef, bone-in (any cut is fine)
2 Tbsp. tomato paste
¼ cup celery, finely chopped
2 Tbsp. olive oil
½ cup brown lentils
½ cup chickpeas canned or cooked
½ cup all-purpose flour
1 cup plain yogurt
Salt and pepper
½ cup short vermicelli
¼ cup fresh cilantro leaves
8 cups water

Directions:

- Heat the oil in a skillet, over medium-high heat and sauté the onions until they become transparent.
- Rinse the meat well and pat dry. Add the meat and tomato paste to the onions, stirring occasionally for 10 minutes.
- Pour in the water and simmer for 15 minutes, until it starts bubbling.
- Add the lentils and chickpeas and simmer until *al dente*.
- Add the celery, red bell pepper, carrots, tomatoes, and chopped cilantro. Simmer on low heat for 30 to 40 minutes.

- In a bowl, combine some of the stock from the pot with plain yogurt and all-purpose flour and mix well. Gradually add the mixture to the soup while stirring. Season with salt and pepper.

Simmer on low heat until it starts bubbling.

- Add the cilantro leaves and short vermicelli. Cook until pasta is fully cooked.

Note:

-Fresh cilantro is similar to fresh Italian flat leaf parsley but the former has a distinctive aroma.

-If short vermicelli is not available, you can use regular vermicelli broken into 1" (2 ½ cm) pieces.

Meatballs Soup

Ingredients:

For the meatballs:

1 ¼ lbs. (½ kg) ground beef or lamb
½ medium onion, finely chopped
1 Tbsp. parsley, finely chopped
1 clove garlic, minced
¼ cup pickled lemon, finely chopped
½ Tbsp. allspice
1 tsp. salt
¼ tsp. black pepper

For the Soup:
2 Tbsp. oil
½ medium onion
2 cloves garlic
6 Tbsp. tomato paste
8 cups stock (chicken or other meat)
½ tsp. paprika
¼ tsp. red hot pepper
¼ cup semolina flour
½ Tbsp. dried mint
Fresh mint for garnish (optional)

Directions:

- Combine the meat, onion, garlic, parsley, and spices. Mix well and form into small balls the size of grapes. Place in a baking pan.
- Bake at 350°F (180°C) until browned, about 15 to 20 minutes. You can also pan- fry them.
- In a skillet, heat the oil and sauté the onion and garlic until they are golden brown.
- Add the tomato paste and stock.
- Mix in the salt, paprika, and hot red pepper. Bring the mixture to a boil.
- Gradually add semolina all-purpose flour, stirring. Cook, stirring constantly, until well combined, about 5 minutes.
- Add the cooked meatballs and return to a boil, then remove from heat.

- Garnish with some dried or fresh mint, as desired.

Note:

Moroccan and Tunisian cuisines are famous for using pickled lemons and olives. The pickles are served only on the side, or incorporated into the dishes.

Picture 14: Meatballs Soup

Harisa Sauce

Ingredients:

1 Tbsp. tomato paste
5 fresh hot chilli peppers
1 cup olive oil
2 cloves garlic, peeled
1 Tbsp. ground cumin
2 Tbsp. Tabasco pepper sauce
2 Tbsp. water
½ tsp. salt

Directions:

- Cut off the stem of the hot chilli pepper and remove the seeds.
- In a small bowl, whisk Tabasco pepper sauce with water until the mixture is transparent.
- Finely chop the garlic with the hot peppers using either a food processor or a mortar and pestle. Add the cumin, salt, and the Tabasco mixture. Pulse or grind until the mixture becomes a thick paste
- In a pan, heat the oil over medium-high heat. Add the spices and the garlic paste, stirring frequently. Add the tomato paste and cook until the mixture becomes a thick sauce.
- Serve hot or cold.

Albisara

This dish is famous in North Africa. It is made from dry fava beans which are soaked and shelled. It is served hot or cold with olive oil and lemons.

Ingredients:

2 cups dry fava beans
2 medium onions, chopped
½ cup onions, thinly sliced into strips
2 cloves garlic
6 cups water
½ cup celery, chopped
1 Tbsp. cilantro, chopped
1 Tbsp. parsley, chopped
1 tsp. dry mint, or
¼ cup fresh mint, chopped
1 Tbsp. vegetable oil
Salt and pepper

Directions:

- Rinse the fava beans. Soak for 8 hours, and then rinse with cold water and shell.
- In a pot, combine the water, fava beans, and the rest of the ingredients except 1 Tbsp. of oil and the onions.
- Simmer the mixture on low heat for 2 hours without stirring. Add extra water when necessary. Skim the surface frequently until the mixture is clear.
- When the fava beans are soft, mash by hand or blend in a food processor. Return to the saucepan and cook over medium-high heat until the mixture is thick.
- *Albisara* is served hot or cold. For garnish, heat the oil over medium-high heat and caramelize the onions until golden brown. Transfer to a plate lined with paper towels. Garnish *Albisara* with the onions and slices of lemon if desired.

Note:

-*Albisara* can be garnished with cooked ground meat in place of caramelized onions. Similarly, chicken stock or meat stock can be used in place of water.

Picture 15: Albisara

Trshi Pickles

Ingredients:

3 cups water
1 cup vinegar
3 Tbsp. salt
½ head cauliflower
1 red bell pepper
1 large carrot
1 stalk celery
10 pepperoncini

Picture 16: Trshi Pickles

Directions :

- In a pot, bring to a boil the water, vinegar, and salt over medium-high heat. Remove from heat and set aside to cool.
- Peel the carrots and cut into coins. A serrated knife can be used to give them a ridged form.
- Chop the celery. Slice the red bell pepper and cut the cauliflower into bite-sized florets.
- In a jar, press all the vegetables in layers. Add the water and vinegar brine. Cover securely and set aside for one week.
- Keep in the refrigerator after opening the jar.

Note:

Select equal-sized, medium cucumbers for pickling.

Cabbage and Turnip Pickles

When combined with beets, cabbage picks up a very attractive color due to it's ability to absorb colors.

Ingredients:

1 or more medium Turnip, peeled and chopped into cubes or rounds
2 ¼ lbs. (1 kg) cabbage, about a small head
7 cups water
4 Tbsp. salt
½ cup white vinegar

Directions:

- Shred the cabbage or cut the head into quarters. Rinse well and add 2 Tbsp of salt.
- Let the cabbage stand in the strainer for several hours to drain water.
- Rinse the salt from cabbage. In a jar, press the cabbage and Turnips into layers.
- Dissolve salt in water and vinegar and pour brine over the layered vegetable until completely covered. Seal the jar securely.
- Set aside for one week before using. Refrigerate once the jar is open.

Picture 17: Cabbage and Turnip Pickles